Our WILD™ WORLD
SERIES

Wild Horses

NORTHWORD
Minnetonka, Minnesota

To Carl and Emma, with love from Aunt Julie—J. V.

Photography © 2004: Michael H. Francis: cover, pp. 8, 15, 16, 17, 21, 26, 38-39, 40, 43, 44; Jeff Vanuga: pp. 4, 5, 18-19, 22, 31, 42; Bill Lea/BillLea.com: p. 12; Dominique Braud: back cover, pp. 11, 25, 28, 32, 35, 36.

Illustrations by Mike Rowe
Designed by Russell S. Kuepper
Edited by Kristen McCurry
Front cover image: Wild horses (*Equus caballus*), Bighorn Canyon National Recreation Area

NorthWord
11571 K-Tel Drive
Minnetonka, MN 55343
1-888-255-9989
www.tnkidsbooks.com

Library of Congress Cataloging-in-Publication Data

Vogel, Julia.
  Wild horses / Julia Vogel ; illustrations by Mike Rowe.
    p. cm. – (Our wild world series)
  Summary: Details the natural history, life cycle, physical characteristics, habitat, diet, and mating of wild horses through-
  out the world.
  ISBN 1-55971-881-1 (hc) – ISBN 1-55971-882-X (sc)
    1. Wild horses—Juvenile literature. [1. Wild horses. 2. Horses.] I. Rowe, Mike (Mike L.), ill. II. Title. III. Series.

SF360.V65 2004
599.665'5—dc22

                                                          2003059973

Printed in Malaysia

CPSIA Tracking Information:
Selangor Darul Ehsan Malaysia
Date of Production: August 2011
Cohort: Batch # 1

Wild Horses

Julia Vogel
Illustrations by Mike Rowe

NorthWord
Minnetonka, Minnesota

LONG AGO all horses were wild animals. They ran free in large herds, or groups, across vast grasslands all over the world. In North America's Great Plains, millions of horses once roamed alongside bison, antelope, and other prairie wildlife.

Today, most horses are cared for by their owners. But untamed horses, often called mustangs, still live in remote parts of the American West, far away from most communities. Wild horses also live in a few other places in the United States and around the world. No one brings them food and water or protects them from danger. How do these last wild horses survive on their own?

Wild horses must be able to survive in bitter winter cold and fierce summer heat.

Strong bones and powerful muscles allow wild horses to run faster than any of their natural enemies.

Mustangs belong to a group of large mammals known as the equid (EH-kwid) family. Zebras, wild asses, and burros are also equids. Horses and their close relatives share body features that help them stay alive in open spaces. Long necks help them spot enemies far away, and long legs help them run fast to escape. On each foot, equids have only one toe, protected by a hard covering, or hoof. Hooves help make horses fast and sure-footed, allowing them to stand, walk, and even gallop on their tiptoes.

Almost 60 million years ago, tiny ancestors (AN-sess-torz) of today's equids lived in North America. The fox-sized animals, called dawn horses, ate leaves in swamps and wet forests. As time passed, the climate grew drier and prairies replaced many woodlands. Fossils show that early horses changed, too. They developed longer legs and necks, plus harder teeth that let them eat tough grasses. By about three million years ago, horses looked very much like they do today.

Wild Horses
FUNFACT:

Horses run free in many countries, including Argentina, Australia, China, France, Poland, and Canada.

The earliest horses traveled through swampy woodlands on paw-like feet,
with four toes on each front foot and three toes on each back foot.

Burros have longer ears and stockier bodies than their horse cousins. Gold miners brought burros to the U.S. as pack animals, and about 4,000 still roam free in the West.

For thousands of years, wild horses crossed land bridges that connected North America to other continents. Horses spread widely across Europe, Asia, Africa, and South America. At the end of the last Ice Age, melting ice packs raised sea levels and flooded the land bridges. The wild horses could no longer cross between continents and had to stay wherever they had traveled. About 8,000 to 10,000 years ago, many large mammals died out in North and South America. Horses, along with mastodons (MASS-ta-dons), camels, and woolly mammoths, vanished mysteriously.

Climate change, disease, and hunting by native people may each have played a part in their disappearance. Whatever the cause, North America's prairies lost their horses.

No one knows where or when people first domesticated (doh-MESS-tih-KATE-ed), or tamed, horses. Cave paintings in France show that Europeans in the Ice Age hunted wild horses for meat. However, by 4,000 to 3,000 B.C., horses in Europe and Asia were valued as work animals as well as for their meat, hides, and milk. People used horses to pull chariots across the grassy plains of eastern Europe and the deserts of the Middle East. Soon the strongest horses were carrying warriors into battle, packing supplies up mountains, and hauling farm wagons. The swiftest horses delivered messages and news faster than ever before. Fast horses were also used for entertainment, including chariot races in the 680 B.C. Olympics.

As people used horses for more and more tasks, they chose the animals that were best at each job and mated, or bred, them to produce even better offspring. Horses were bred to improve qualities such as strength, speed, color, jumping ability, and personality. Careful breeding over the centuries led to the creation of many different breeds, or varieties, of horses. Scientists group all tame horses in the same species (SPEE-sees), *Equus caballus*, just as all dogs belong to the same species, *Canis familiaris*. But the many breeds can look remarkably different. Horse breeds now range in size from the Falabella miniature pony, which may weigh only 31 pounds (14 kg) to the Belgian draft horse, which can reach 2,400 pounds (1,090 kg).

People continued to hunt the remaining herds of wild horses for meat and sport. By the late 1800s, a group of horses in Mongolia called Przewalski's (psha-VALL-skeez) horses were the last remaining true wild horses. A few were captured to keep in zoos, but no one was ever able to tame the fiesty animals. Although the wild herds of these horses died out in the 1900s, groups of Przewalski's horses raised by people have now been set free in Mongolia.

No horses, wild or tame, lived in North America for at least 8,000 years.

When the animals finally returned, they were the tame horses ridden by Spanish conquistadors (kon-KEES-ta-dorz). These strong, swift animals carried the armed soldiers through jungles and across deserts in search of gold. In the 1600s, Spanish settlers raised their tough little horses on cattle and sheep ranches in New Mexico. Some ranch horses escaped to live in the wild. The free-running horses came to be called "mustangs," probably from the Spanish word *mesteño* (mess-TEN-yo), which means stray or free-running animal.

Wild Horses
FUNFACT:

The very first horses brought back to America were 16 Spanish horses that landed in Mexico with the conquistadors in 1519.

In the windswept Mongolian grasslands, the wild Przewalski's horse is known as takhi.

Spanish colonists, farmers, and others set horses free on several islands along the Atlantic coast. Though surrounded by salt water, these islands often have little of the freshwater and grasses that horses need to survive.

Some Spanish horses were stolen by Pueblos and other Native Americans. Plains Indians called the unknown creatures "sky dogs" or "elk dogs" and quickly learned to hunt bison and attack enemies on horseback. Trading, theft, and captures from the wild herds helped spread mustangs to northern groups of Native Americans, such as the Dakota and Blackfoot. Many of their horses escaped, too, and the free herds thrived on the lush prairie grasses of the northern plains.

Later European settlers brought different kinds of horses to the prairies, such as heavy draft breeds to pull farm equipment. Some broke free and joined the wild herds. Though the wild horses were no longer all pure Spanish horses, even the mixed-breed animals were usually called "mustangs." The wild herds grew to about two million animals by the mid 1800s.

Throughout the 19th century, wild horses were still often caught and tamed. Captured horses became riding horses, cow ponies, pack animals, and U.S. Cavalry mounts. In the early 20th century, though, people needed fewer horses. They began to value wild horses less. Many argued that the animals were not pure Spanish horses but mongrels, or mixed breeds that were no longer useful or important. In fact, some said wild horses were not native wildlife but feral, or stray, animals that did not belong on the prairies. Some ranchers blamed the horses for competing with their cattle for water and range grass. Some hunters believed that mustangs ate the food of elk, bighorn sheep, and other wildlife they wanted to hunt. Horses were chased off and fenced out of the best grasslands with barbed wire. Thousands were rounded up and sold for pet food or shot as pests. Their numbers fell to 17,000 before they were protected by a 1971 U.S. law. This law banned capturing, harming, or killing free-roaming horses or burros on public lands.

Today, about 50,000 wild horses live in the U.S. and Canada. Some live on private ranches, wildlife refuges, or Native American reservations. A few small groups live on islands off the East Coast, in Georgia, Maryland, North Carolina, Virginia, and Nova Scotia. Most are found on publicly owned land in western states, especially Nevada and Wyoming. Nearly all wild horses live in rugged, dry habitats, or natural environments, where they must work hard to survive.

Because of their harsh habitats, wild horses are smaller than many other kinds of horses. Adults stand about 56 inches (142 cm) high at the shoulder, the height of a tall pony breed. A large male mustang, called a stallion (STAL-yun), weighs at most 1,000 pounds (454 kg). A small female, or mare (MAYR), may weigh only 650 pounds (295 kg). At that size, mustangs grow strong on poor lands where larger domestic horses might starve.

With ancestors from many breeds, wild horses come in many colors and patterns. Most common are different shades of brown, from golden to chestnut to almost black. Horses with brown bodies and black manes, tails, and lower legs are called bays. Black, gray, and tan are other common mustang colors. Roan (ROWN) horses are black or brown with white hairs sprinkled through their coats, and pintos have patches of white and black or brown. A few boldly patterned horses appear to have white blankets with dark spots across their rumps. Those mustangs are called Appaloosas and may be related to horses bred by the Nez Percé Indians long ago.

Wild Horses
FUNFACT:

One coat pattern, called Medicine Hat pinto, was especially valued by some Native Americans. They believed the horses' special coat pattern protected the animals and their riders from battle injuries.

The coat pattern of every pinto is unique, and some Native Americans treasured these flashy mustangs over horses of other colors and patterns.

About 150 to 200 horses with scientifically proven Spanish ancestry live in the Pryor Mountain Wild Horse Range of Wyoming and Montana.

A few mustangs have even more unusual markings, with zebra-like stripes on their legs, and a stripe down the spine. These rare horses often have short backs with one less vertebra (VER-tih-bruh), or backbone, than other horses. Early Spanish breeds and other ancient types of horses had these same traits. A group of these mustangs live in the Pryor Mountains of Montana and Wyoming. Blood tests show that these horses are closely related to their Spanish ancestors of 400 years ago. Scientists believe this is because the mountains isolated these horses, or kept them from mixing with other breeds.

Even in the desert, wild horses cannot live far from streams or other sources of fresh water.

The Pryor Mountain mustangs are now carefully protected and are considered an important part of Western U.S. history.

Wild horses need lots of water to drink. In the driest country, they can go two or three days without water. Horses prefer to drink every day, usually about 10 to 15 gallons (38 to 57 liters). In winter, they eat snow or use their hard hooves to break through pond ice. In hot weather, they stay close to water holes and drink more often if possible. Water is so important to horses that droughts (DROWTS), or rainfall shortages, are probably the biggest natural threat to wild herds.

Horses cannot see well close up, so their sense of smell helps them find their favorite grasses.

Horses need food as well as water every day. They are plant-eaters, or herbivores (HERB-uh-vorz). Their favorite foods are grasses, plants with thin leaves and tiny flowers. Other kinds of plant leaves grow from the tip, but grass leaves grow from the base. That means that when horses bite off some grass, the leaves keep growing. After grazing the grass in one area, horses move to fresh pasture. As long as they have plenty of space, wild horses do not overgraze, or harm grass by eating too much of the plants.

Horses eat many kinds of grasses and other plants. Bluebunch wheat grass, Sandburg's bluegrass, and needle-and-thread grass attract them all year. In spring, a mustang may also eat blooms of flowers such as balsam root, or flowering plants such as dandelions and rosy everlasting. In winter, horses must search harder for food. They may nibble the leaves of bitterbrush, rabbitbrush, and other shrubs. If horses get very hungry, they may even eat juniper bark and twigs. An adult mustang eats about 16 to 30 pounds (7 to 14 kg) of food per day.

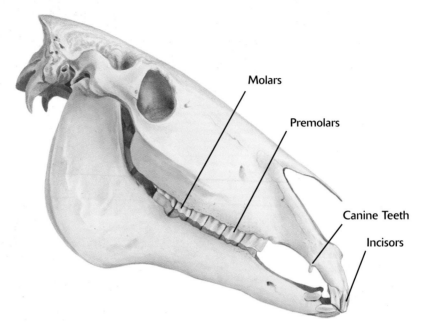

Molars

Premolars

Canine Teeth

Incisors

The largest bone in a horse's skull is its powerful lower jaw.
An adult horse usually has 40 teeth.

Horses bite grass off close to the ground with chisel-shaped front teeth, called incisors (in-SIZE-orz). Flat-topped back teeth, or molars, thoroughly crush each bite. So much grinding wears down the molars, but a horse's teeth keep growing all its life.

Even well-chewed grass is hard to digest. Cattle, deer, and many other plant-eating mammals have four-chambered stomachs that break down their food. Horses have a one-chambered stomach as humans do, but horses also have a special pouch in their intestines (in-TES-tins), called the cecum (SEE-kem), that aids in digestion (die-JEST-shun). Tiny bacteria (bak-TEER-ee-uh) live in the cecum. Once the swallowed grass reaches the cecum, bacteria break it down so the horse's body can absorb the nutrition (new-TRISH-un). This digestive system means that horses can live in dry lands with poor quality grasses. However, they must eat more food than cattle of the same size to get enough nutrition.

Experts can estimate a horse's age by its teeth. Over time, rough grasses wear down the teeth in specific patterns.

Horses have four natural gaits, or ways of moving: walk, trot, canter, and gallop, which is the fastest.

Whether grazing or resting, wild horses must stay alert for predators (PRED-uh-torz). A mountain lion may be crouching behind a boulder, or a black bear may be lumbering through the trees. If cornered by a pack of coyotes, an adult horse can defend itself with powerful kicks. Predators most often attack foals, or horses less than a year old. A mare could try to defend her young, but usually both run. If the foal cannot keep up, it may be doomed.

Horses are built for speed and nearly always run from danger. A mustang's top speed, 35 miles per hour (56 km per hour), makes it faster than any of its natural enemies. Horses also can leap over obstacles, such as fallen logs or

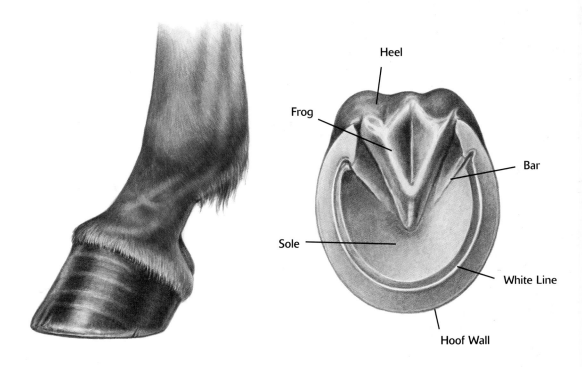

Heel

Frog

Bar

Sole

White Line

Hoof Wall

Like its teeth, a horse's hooves wear down
with so much use but keep growing all its life.

broad ditches, and make sudden turns and zigzags. If a river blocks their way, horses can swim to safety.

Scrambling through rocks, mustangs are amazingly surefooted. At the back of a horse's foot is a wedge-shaped, springy pad called a frog. The frog cushions the hoof and protects the leg as it strikes hard surfaces. The small pad can be life saving, because a wild horse with a broken leg will not survive. With their shock-absorbing frogs and hard hooves, mustangs could outrun a champion racehorse on rocky ground. Mustangs are also famous for their stamina (STAM-ih-nuh), which means they can keep running long after other animals must stop to rest.

Horses rely on their keen senses to warn them of danger. They have large eyes that are very sensitive to movement and can see far into the distance. Positioned on the sides of the head, the eyes take in a broad field of view. A horse can move each eye separately, so the animal can watch in front and behind at the same time. They do not see colors as people do, but they see better in the dark than humans. Horses sometimes seem nervous and jumpy to observers, but their eyes may be telling them of possible dangers humans cannot see.

Horses also have sharp hearing. Their cup-shaped ears collect sound from near and far. Like their eyes, their ears can move separately. A horse can turn its ears in almost any direction without moving its head. If a mustang hears something frightening, it may bolt without ever looking to see what made the sound.

Horses also have a surprisingly sensitive sense of touch. When a biting fly lands on its skin, a mustang reacts fast. It twitches its skin, swishes its tail, and even shakes its whole body to get rid of the pests. Pairs of horses may stand side-by-side, head-to-tail, helping each other swish away flies. To protect their skin and perhaps soothe bites, horses roll in dirt or mud. On hot days when insects are worst, mustangs climb to high country in search of winds to blow the swarms away.

Owners of domestic horses care for their horses' skin by daily grooming, or brushing and combing. Wild horses groom each other. A pair stands together, each partner nibbling the other's mane and coat, especially around the shoulders. Horses groom each other for just a few minutes, but they often stay together afterward. Grooming and other touching seems to help horses get along.

Getting along matters because horses are highly social animals. Mustangs almost always live together, usually in small groups called bands. A typical family band is made up of one mature (ma-TOOR) stallion, one to eight mares, and their offspring under two or three years old. The mares in a family band are often called a harem.

The band stallion constantly protects his family from danger. He often stands apart from the rest, alert while the others graze. Stallions can rarely snatch more than a mouthful of grass or a few minutes of sleep. At the first sign of trouble, the stallion snorts a loud warning.

He may circle the group, nipping at slow mares and foals, hurrying them to join the others. Then the band members dash away, but the stallion stops to look back, ready to fight if necessary.

To a wild stallion, the worst kind of trouble may be another male mustang. Rivals try to sneak up on the band and steal a mare or two, or the whole harem. When a challenger approaches, both stallions prance and toss their heads, sniff noses, paw the ground, and squeal. Usually after less than a minute, one horse gallops away, defeated. Such sparring teaches the stallions in an area who is strongest.

Wild Horses
FUNFACT:

A stallion is usually not powerful enough to take over a band until at least age five.

Stallions use teeth, hooves, and bodies as weapons during short, fierce battles. The winner rounds up one or more mares and takes them away.

Serious fights are rare, but if neither horse backs off, a fierce battle breaks out. Both males rear back on their hind legs and strike out with their front hooves. They lunge at each other, biting at legs, sides, and necks. This pawing and turning kicks up so much dust that it is hard to see the action. These battles are noisy, with angry neighs (NAYZ) and dull thuds whenever their bodies slam together. At last one horse gives up, leaving the other with the band. Each may have bloody wounds, torn ears, or other scars that last a lifetime.

This band has spread out to graze, but all will fall into line behind the lead mare when she decides it's time to move.

During the battles, mares often graze quietly nearby. The outcome seems to matter little to the band. Mares have their own leader, an older female who is almost as bossy as the band stallion. The lead mare gets to drink first at water holes and picks where the band eats each day. When the stallion snorts an alarm, band members instantly follow the lead mare to safety. All trust her to choose an escape route that is fast but not too difficult for the youngest foals. Their lives depend on her knowledge and quick thinking.

The whole band must communicate well to keep safe. Horses make several kinds of sounds. Each horse has a unique call, or neigh, that other band members recognize. Mustangs also whinny, a loud call that can be heard far away. If one horse gets separated from the rest, it whinnies and listens for the band to answer. When any horse snorts, the others lift their heads and watch out for danger. But a soft nicker reassures the other animals that all is well. A nicker is a quiet, throaty noise like a soft chuckle. Mares use nickers especially as tender greetings for their foals.

Wild Horses
FUNFACT:

Horses can sleep lying down or standing up. Their legs lock so they can relax without falling over.

Alert   Sleepy   Angry

A horse's ears, eyes, and nostrils help communicate its mood to other band members.

Body language also helps mustangs communicate. Feet, tails, and ears give clues to mustang moods. Stomping a front hoof is a mild warning, telling others to step back. Holding up a back hoof declares, "I am about to kick!" Normally, a horse's tail hangs down in a relaxed position. An excited horse may lift its tail into the air as it trots or prances. If a horse nervously flicks its tail back and forth, it is a sign of anger.

A horse communicates with its ears, too. An alert horse pricks its ears forward or turns them back and forth. A sleepy horse's ears droop. If the ears flatten back against the horse's head it means the mustang is angry and may bite or kick.

A foal nurses while its mother stays alert to danger.
A mare almost never gives birth to more than one foal at a time.

Mares do not always get along, but they rarely leave the band. Stallions may let mares go off alone to give birth. Sometime in April, May, or June, a mare ready to give birth looks for a quiet spot hidden from mountain lions and other predators. The foal arrives feet first. The new mother nuzzles it, getting to know its smell, and nickers softly. Soon, the newborn starts untangling its stilt-like legs, struggling to stand. A healthy foal stands up within an hour of birth and soon nudges under its mother's belly to nurse, or drink its mother's milk. Any foal too injured or weak to walk will be left behind when its mother returns to the band.

Adult horses usually only run when startled, but foals like this one run to build muscles and to play with other foals.

A young male horse is called a colt until it is four years old, and a young female is called a filly. Newborn colts and fillies weigh around 66 pounds (30 kg). Like adult mustangs, their coat colors and patterns vary. Mare and foal rejoin the band a day or so after the birth, sticking close together. The foal nurses several times a day at first, but it starts nibbling grass at three to four weeks. By its first winter, most of its nutrition comes from grass. Mares usually wean, or stop nursing, their yearling offspring shortly before new foals arrive the next spring.

Throughout their first year, colts and fillies play hard. They race each other, kick up their heels, and nip at their parents and older siblings. Sometimes, their play annoys older band members. Then the foals clack their teeth, a sound that seems to say, "Sorry! Please don't kick me!" Their rough play helps the foals grow strong. Perhaps even more important, they develop close relationships that hold the band together.

Wild Horses
FUNFACT:

A horse's height is often measured in "hands."
One hand is equal to 4 inches (10 cm), and
an adult mustang usually stands about
14 hands (142 cm) at the shoulder.

A filly stays with her family until she is one or two years old, when an outside stallion usually steals her away. After fillies leave and join new bands, many have their own foals by the next spring. The band stallion usually chases a colt out of the band when the young male is one or two. Band stallions do not welcome new colts, and the young males are not yet strong enough to take over bands of mares. Instead, they join another kind of horse group called a bachelor (BACH-ler) band. Bands of 2 to 12 young male mustangs stick together for safety and comfort.

The bachelors lead carefree lives. Like other mustangs, they spend much of each day and night seeking food and water. But unlike band stallions, they have time to rest and play. Sometimes they chase other bachelors as if they were harem mares. Or they rear and paw the air at each other in mock battles. Such play helps them build skills they will need to take over their own family bands in the future.

These three bachelor stallions are dun colored, a common coat pattern for wild horses with Spanish mustang ancestors. They live together in Oregon's Kiger Horse Management Area.

Even if a stallion like this pinto has only one mare, he guards her constantly.

Bachelor bands and family bands sometimes join into a large herd. Usually, herds gather briefly in areas with good grass and plentiful water. Young males keep to the edges, while band stallions watch them nervously and keep their mares tightly bunched. Within the herd, some stallions rank above others. Bands with the most powerful males get the best grass and the first chance to drink at water holes. In the past, herds sometimes included thousands of horses. Today few areas have enough wild horses to form herds of even 100.

In large and small groups, mustangs' lives are shaped by the seasons. Every spring foals arrive, and mares mate again just days after giving birth. Summer brings blazing heat in prairies and deserts, and the animals must find ways to stay cool. They roll in cool mud at water holes and rest in the shade of any trees or boulders they can find. They also must stay alert for wildfires, using their noses to test the wind. A sniff of smoke warns, "Wildfire! Run!"

Wild horses do not migrate long distances between summer and winter territories. Instead, many migrate to different elevations, climbing up or down, depending on the season. In summer, they seek cool breezes and fresh grass by climbing to mountain meadows. They walk to get water in the coolest parts of the day and graze more often at night.

Wild Horses
FUNFACT:

In the past, the biggest mustang herds lived in Texas.
Some early Texas maps had large areas simply
labeled, "Vast herds of wild horses."

By fall, horses are growing thick coats for cold-weather protection. Bands come down from mountains or high ground to wind-sheltered valleys. The first snows bring hardships, forcing mustangs to dig for food and break ice for water. Older horses remember where to find grass and shrubs, and foals follow them, learning where to look and how to dig. During the winter, bands spend nearly all their time just finding enough to eat. Blizzards may drive the horses to huddle together behind evergreen trees for warmth, and ice storms may prevent them from eating at all. By spring, the survivors' ribs show through their patchy, shedding coats. All are eager to taste the first green shoots of spring grass.

Despite their hard lives, mustangs have long life spans. They can live over 20 years in the wild. A family band's mares may stay together until they die. A band stallion, though, only stays as long as he can drive off challengers.

The first snowfall is a sign that the wild bands should move to sheltered pastures.

Thick coats help this yearling (left) and its mother survive winter in the Pryor Mountain Range. The mare's rounded belly shows she may be expecting a new foal in the spring.

Defeated older stallions do not join bachelor bands but live alone. Unless they can steal or win new mares, these stallions never father offspring again. Without other horses for companionship and safety, they may not survive long.

With long life spans and with most mares having new foals every year, wild horse herds can grow quickly. In fact, they can double in size in four or five years. Too many grazing animals could harm the horses' dry habitat because it kills grasses, erodes soil, and pollutes streams with churned-up mud and droppings. The worst overgrazing can cause desertification (de-ZERT-if-ih-KAY-shun), or the changing of rich grassland into unhealthy desert.

This young foal must feel safe enough to lie down and rest.
Soon it will be up and running free again.

Mustangs share the range with over four million livestock and two million antelope, elk, and other large wild animals. Ecologists, or scientists who study natural systems, are working to learn how horses and other plant-eating animals affect the land.

Are there too many wild horses? To prevent overgrazing, a federal agency called the Bureau (BYUR-oh) of Land Management studies herd size on public lands. Herds that the Bureau thinks are growing too fast are rounded up, and many of the horses are offered to the public for adoption. Unwanted horses, often older animals, may be released again or sent to live on private mustang sanctuaries (SANK-choo-air-ees), or protected places.

Roundups, though, are expensive and can frighten or injure horses. A better solution may be to give mustangs a kind of medicine that reduces their ability to have offspring. The horses do not need to be rounded up to get the medicine, making controlling horse populations less expensive and less stressful for the horses.

Like other prairie animals, mustangs need open spaces. Wild horses are symbols of freedom, reminders of Spanish explorers, bold Native Americans, and dashing cowboys. Most of all, they are free creatures, adapted to life on their own. Mustangs do need our help, though, to make sure there are always wild lands where they can run free.

Internet Sites

You can find out more interesting information about wild horses and lots of other wildlife by visiting these Internet sites.

Animal Nation
www.animalnation.com

Black Hills Wild Horse Sanctuary
www.wildmustangs.com

Bureau of Land Management
www.blm.gov/education/00_resources/articles/wild_bunch/index.html

Foundation for the Protection and Preservation of the Przewalski Horse
www.treemail.nl/takh/

Horse Behavior
www.horse-behavior.com/index.html

Kentucky Horse Park
www.imh.org

National Geographic.com for Kids
www.nationalgeographic.com/kids/creature_feature/0204/horses.html

PBS
www.net.unl.edu/artsFeat/wildhorses

Shackleford Bank Horses
www.shacklefordhorses.org

Peoples Trust for the Environment
enc.org.uk/

alzoo.si.edu/publications/zoogoer/1997/5/equidprimer.cfm

Index

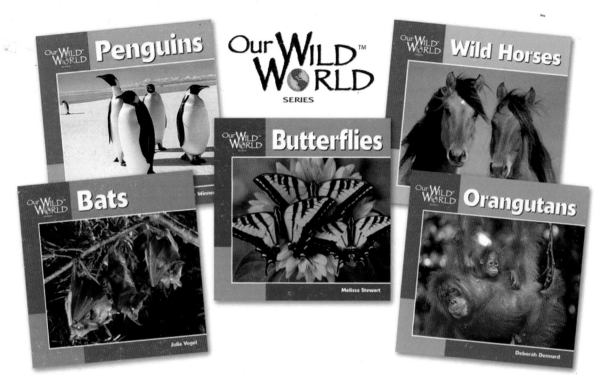

Titles available in the Our Wild World Series:

NorthWord
Minnetonka, Minnesota